No Boredom Allowed!

Paper Bead Crafts

written by
Florence Quinn

illustrated by
Jessica Dacher

STERLING

New York / London

www.sterlingpublishing.com/kids

STERLING and the distinctive Sterling logo are registered trademarks of
Sterling Publishing Co., Inc.

Library of Congress Cataloging-in-Publication Data

Quinn, Florence.
No boredom allowed. Paper bead crafts / Florence Quinn ; illustrated by Jessica Dacher.
p. cm.
ISBN 978-1-4027-5037-3
1. Beadwork—Juvenile literature. 2. Paper work—Juvenile literature.
I. Dacher, Jessica. II. Title. III. Title: Paper bead crafts.
TT860.Q95 2008
745.58'2--dc22
2008013764

2 4 6 8 10 9 7 5 3 1

Published by Sterling Publishing Co., Inc.
387 Park Avenue South, New York, NY 10016
© 2008 by Sterling Publishing Co., Inc.
Illustrations © 2008 by Jessica Dacher
Distributed in Canada by Sterling Publishing
c/o Canadian Manda Group, 165 Dufferin Street
Toronto, Ontario, Canada M6K 3H6
Distributed in the United Kingdom by GMC Distribution Services
Castle Place, 166 High Street, Lewes, East Sussex, England BN7 1XU
Distributed in Australia by Capricorn Link (Australia) Pty. Ltd.
P.O. Box 704, Windsor, NSW 2756, Australia

Manufactured in the United States of America

Sterling ISBN 978-1-4027-5037-3

For information about custom editions, special sales, premium and
corporate purchases, please contact Sterling Special Sales
Department at 800-805-5489 or specialsales@sterlingpublishing.com.

contents

Joe
Donidson

Fast Fashion

So, you've never thought of making jewelry out of paper? Fantastic! This book is going to teach you just how to do that—and more. There are tons of funky things you can make out of paper beads: jewelry, of course, but also ornaments, decorations, bookmarks, and key chains.

Impress your friends with unique gifts that you've made with your own two hands. Create a buzz at school tomorrow when you walk into class wearing a one-of-a-kind original. Remind yourself how artistic you are each time you finish a chapter of that book you're reading. You can even help decorate your family's home with cool ornaments you've made. It's simple, totally fun, and you don't even need an adult to help you.

This book is all you'll need to start and finish your projects. After the instructions and finishing techniques, you'll find pages and pages of triangular templates that you can color in, cut out, and roll into beads. Some are already designed for you, and some are blank so you can get inspired and create your own. Try out different color combinations, have fun, get crazy—you can even use metallic trimmings if you like.

So get out your markers, pencils, scissors, and glue, and get ready to get creative!

First Things First

Tools you will need:

o   colored pencils, markers,
    crayons, and pens

o   safety scissors

o   newspaper

o   glue stick

o   drinking straw or pencil

o   toothpick

1. Spread some newspaper on your working surface for easy clean-up at the end of your project.

2. Color and design your triangle however you want. Use markers, crayons, colored pencils, even metallic gel pens to get your desired look.

3. Cut out your triangle along the outline.

4. Starting with the wider end of the triangle, roll the paper around a drinking straw or pencil. This will help curl the paper and make it easier to roll up tightly when you make your bead. Remember: The decorated part should be on the outside.

5. Starting again with the wide end of the triangle, roll the paper tightly around a toothpick until you are halfway to the top of the triangle, and stop there. Don't roll the paper so tightly that you can't get it off the toothpick!

6. Using the glue stick, apply glue to the top half of the triangle and continue rolling all the way up. Press down lightly on the part of the triangle that has glue on it, and make sure it sticks well. Let the glue dry, then carefully remove your bead from the toothpick.

7. And there you have it! Repeat these steps until you've made enough beads to complete your project.

Finishing Techniques

Tools you will need:

o Clear nail polish or brush-on glaze medium that is transparent when dry

o Colored nail polish or paint

o String, wire, or thread

o Scissors

o Jewelry clasps and earring hooks

o Safety pins

Once the glue on your beads has dried, you can do all sorts of things to make them look artistic and professional. Remember to work over a protective covering of newspaper so you can easily clean up any mess.

1. Apply clear nail polish or brush-on glaze (you can try matte or gloss finish) to seal and harden the beads. To do this, place the bead once again on the tip of the toothpick you used for rolling. Hold the other end of the toothpick while brushing on

clear nail polish or applying glaze medium. Be sure to use enough to cover the whole bead, and let it dry completely. Wait at least 20 minutes for it to dry. You can put the bottom end of the toothpick into something like a potato or a pincushion to hold it upright while you're waiting for the polish or glaze to dry.

2. If you wish, you can use colored nail polish or paint to further decorate your beads. You must also let this dry completely before proceeding with your project.

3. If you use paint for Step 2, apply a second coat of clear glaze in the same manner. If you use colored nail polish, there is no need to add another layer of glaze since the colored nail polish also acts as a glaze. Wait again until your bead has dried completely before going to the next step.

4. Put your beads on thread or string, or stack them onto safety pins. You can make necklaces, bracelets, key chains, and earrings. There are so many cool things you can do with your beads once you have finished making them! The next section will give you some ideas for completing your paper bead projects.

Safety Tips!

1. Cover all project surfaces with newspaper and wear an old T-shirt that covers your clothes. Don't let any of your materials get on furniture or fabrics.

2. Work in a well-ventilated area when you use paint, glue, or finishing medium.

3. Tell an adult in charge what you are doing, just in case you need help.

4. Wash your hands after you finish using paint, glue, and finishing medium—before you do anything else!

Finish It Up!

There are so many cool things you can do with your beads once you finish making them! This section will give you some ideas for completing your paper bead projects.

Earrings: You can buy thin wire, string, fastening clasps, and earring hooks (or clip-ons if you don't have pierced ears) at most bead and craft shops. Make sure you cut enough thin wire or string for your work. Fasten it to the loop at the bottom of the earring hook by bending or tying it. Next, place your beads on the wire or string in the pattern you like and securely fasten the wire or string at the bottom so the beads won't fall off. You can also fasten the wire or string at the top near the earring hook loop to make hoop earrings. Another way to make earrings is by stacking your beads onto a large safety pin and then pinning it to the earring hook loop. You can also get a little more creative and make up your own way to do it!

Necklaces and Bracelets: Again, make sure you have enough thin wire or string to make a necklace or bracelet that will fit you (and give yourself a little extra, too). String your beads in the pattern you like. Fasten the beads by tying knots at either end of your string, and then tie the ends of your beautiful strand to a clasp and wear it proudly! You can also make an anklet or a sunglasses strap this way.

Rings: You'll probably need only one bead for this, especially if you have small fingers. String is the easiest to use for this project, so you can adjust the ring size as necessary. All you have to do is loop a bead onto the string and tie big knots at both ends of the bead to secure it. Unless you can do this one-handed, have someone else tie it to your finger and cut the excess string, then stare at the dazzling thing!

Pins/brooches: You can get very creative with this project and use your beads to make all sorts of designs, like flowers, stars, or anything else. String your beads onto wire to make something stunning, then glue it to a pin back. You can also make barrettes this way by gluing your creation onto a plain barrette clasp. As usual, let your project dry completely. All your fashionable friends will love it, and they'll beg you to make them one.

There are many other things you can decorate or make with your beads:
o   picture frames
o   key chains
o   bookmarks
o   napkin rings
o   Christmas ornaments
o   curtain tiebacks
o   charms

Just use your skills and what you've learned from these instructions, and go paperbead crazy!

Now Design your own!